AF264851

25/

Stace

A

COMPLETE GUIDE

TO THE

ORNAMENTAL

LEATHER WORK.

Entered at Stationers' Hall.

LONDON:

PUBLISHED BY J. REVELL, 272 OXFORD STREET;

SOLD BY

T. T. LEMARE, OXFORD ARMS PASSAGE,
PATERNOSTER ROW;

B. SMITH, 107, FLEET STREET; AND ALL BOOKSELLERS.

Half-a-Crown.

REVELL'S

COMPLETE GUIDE

TO THE

ORNAMENTAL LEATHER WORK.

GENERAL REMARKS.

WE feel assured that a long introduction is neither requisite to the reader or publisher of a Work like the present, and shall, therefore, merely say, that the great success our former little Works have met with, has induced us to send forth this edition, in which will be found every particular connected with this very useful source of amusement and fashionable department of *practical art.* The illustrations are furnished by a late pupil of the School of Design, who obtained the highest prize for Flower Painting, assisted by a student of the ROYAL ACADEMY OF ARTS. Every example given has been practically tested, and, in most instances, the drawings have been copied from the models executed in leather, and will be found to combine durability with beauty of design. In order to make the leather modelling as durable as possible, we have not departed from nature in the finished form, but in the mode of construction; for example, we make several portions of a flower in one piece of leather. The Narcissus and the beautiful White Lily have each six petals; in both instances, we make the entire corolla of the flowers in one piece; thereby, while losing none of the beauty of the natural form of the flowers, we gain strength and solidity; as, were the petals of the Lily or Narcissus to be composed of six pieces, one, if imperfectly cemented, might fall off and detract from the beauty of the entire piece of work. By our method of proceeding, it is impossible to do so : we mention this, as, in our description of Making and Modelling Flowers in Leather, we differ from the literally botanic construction, while, at the same time, we arrive at perfectly correct and artistic formation.

In some flowers, as in the Hop, Dahlia, &c., we have found it impracticable to combine many petals in one piece of leather; where this is the case, especial care must be taken to have good liquid glue, and fasten each petal securely.

All leather to be used in Modelling Leaves, Flowers, &c., must be first wetted, and modelled while wet ; and as this is a general rule, the student will understand that mention of the necessity of this operation will not in every instance be repeated.

Amongst the many uses to which Leather Work is applied, that of ornamenting Pulpits will be found a capital field for the display of this art, as it is capable of being moulded into any form, and nothing can possibly have a more substantial and beautiful appearance.

Glasses of varied form, as jelly glasses and old-fashioned goblets, as well as many of modern manufacture, can be covered on the outside with Leather Work. Lilies of the Valley, and other such flowers, being trailled round a groundwork of leaves, and being either gilded or stained, look exceedingly well; and as they are capable of holding water, become really useful as well as ornamental articles for bouquets of flowers.

Fire-screens and scroll work are executed exactly in the same manner, as described in the following pages, for frames. Fire-screens are generally filled with Berlin wool, or some other fancy work. Those who would prefer to have an entire piece of Leather Work, can paint landscapes or flowers upon white leather, using the same medium which is used at the School of Design for body colour painting, mixed with finely powdered colours.

Gold Leather Work looks remarkably well upon a blue or crimson velvet ground, and makes very rich frames, fire screens, &c. When tastefully arranged, the flowers and leaves upon these grounds have a very magnificent appearance.

Amongst the numerous articles which admit of being ornamented with leather, may be enumerated frames, brackets, vases, pole and hand screens, card plates and racks, music and watch stands.

Revell's Complete Guide to Ornamental Leather Work.

THE MATERIALS.

The principal Materials required for this work are—

Basil Leather.

Skiver ditto.

A Bottle of Oak Varnish Stain.

Ditto Spirit Stain.

Ditto Shaw's Liquid Glue.

A Bottle of Stiffening.

A Small Hammer.

A few Brushes,

Some Tacks.

A pair of Nippers.

A Veining Tool.

A few hard Steel Pens.

Bradawl.

Pair of Scissors.

A Leather-cutting Knife.

Grape Moulds.

Ditto for Passion Flowers.

Fine Black Lead Pencil.

LEATHER.

—

The kind of leather used for general purposes is basil; it should be selected of an even texture and of a light colour, as the lighter coloured basil takes the oak varnish stain better than the dark.

Great care must be taken to select it soft and free from blemishes, as if dark and rough leather is used, the work when finished, even by skilful hands, will not have so good an appearance as the production of much less skilful artists, where good basil leather is used.

The skiver leather is used for making grapes, or very small leaves and flowers, and can be obtained at the same place as the basil leather; this kind is also very useful for thin stems and any minute portion of the work.

DIRECTIONS FOR MAKING THE LEAVES.

Sketch, either from nature, or from the example annexed, the leaf you intend to copy, upon pasteboard ; cut it out very carefully ; then place a piece of basil in

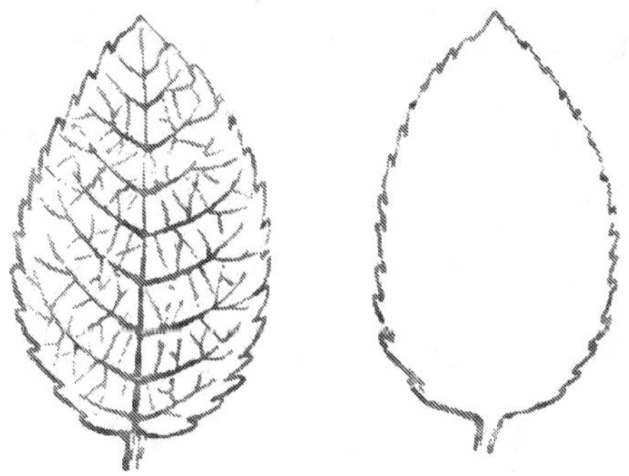

No. 1.

cold water for half a minute (not longer), unless the leather is unusually thick ; the leather should then be taken out of the water, and pressed in a linen cloth until the surface becomes dry.   Being thus prepared, lay it quite flat and place upon it the pasteboard pattern, holding it firmly down with the left hand, while with the right, draw a line round the pattern with a fine hard black lead pencil or the veining tool : while the leather is damp cut out the leaf with a pair of scissors or with the leather-cutting knife, as occasion may require ; when smaller or larger leaves are required, a reduced, or enlarged, sketch should be taken, a pattern made of it in pasteboard, and applied in the same manner as described above, cutting out as many leaves as you require, and generally making about four sizes of them, as varying the sizes of the leaves adds much to the beauty of the foliage. Leaves all the same size would have a very formal appearance, as they must be veined before they are allowed to dry; too much leather must not be wetted at a time, nor more leaves cut out than can be veined. To vein the leaves, mark them with the veining tool on the smooth side of the leather strongly, by pressing heavily on the leaf, where a thick vein is required ; and more lightly where only finer ones should be visible ; for raised veins employ the end of a fine pair of scissors for the large, and a hard steel pen for the

smaller veins.   Being veined, the leaves should be
bent and moulded as they are to appear upon the work
when it is completed: they should then be dried rather
quickly, as it greatly assists in the hardening.

TO HARDEN THEM.

When the leaves are thoroughly dry, brush them all over, particularly the edges with the prepared stiffening, applying it with a camel's hair pencil, nimbly, as it dries very rapidly, apply it thin and evenly, taking care to cover the edges; when dry, they will be ready for staining.

TO STAIN THEM.

Pour a little oak varnish stain into a small vessel, and brush the leaves all over, using a hog's-hair tool for the purpose of laying on the stain, taking care to cover the edges, and brush it well out of the veined parts; should the leaves, when dry, not be so dark as desired, another coat can be given, but in no instance apply thick coats of stain, it will, if put on thick, most likely dry darker in one place than another, and will never have so smooth an appearance as when two thin coats have been applied; take care always that one coat must be dry before another is applied.

TO MAKE STEMS.

Cut strips of basil leather about one-third of an inch wide and as long as the leather will allow ; soak them well in water for a few minutes until they feel very soft, take them out, wipe the water from the surface, then roll them round as tightly as possible (the smooth side outwards) on a table or any even surface, and dry them ; if required very stiff, add inside a piece of wire ; when very thick ones are required the leather must be proportionately wider.

TO MAKE TENDRILLS.

Tendrills are made in the same manner as Stems, using skiver instead of basil leather, dry them quickly, and they will then be ready for use in the following manner: take a tendrill, damp it and immediately wind it round a bradawl or a piece of stout wire, taking care to fasten both ends of the tendrill so that it does not fly off; dry it by the fire, then remove it from the awl and a delicately-formed tendrill will be the result; arrange it and cut to length and form wished, and apply a coat of stiffening to keep it in shape. Stems and tendrills are to be hardened and stained precisely in the same manner as the leaves.

GRAPES.

In order to produce grapes symmetrically formed a proper mould should be obtained; then cut rounds of skiver leather the size required, which must be wetted and placed in the mould the smooth side downwards; then fill the leather in the mould firmly with wadding, and tie the grapes securely with strong thread or fine twine; when the grape is finished, put a piece of wire through the part where it has been tied up to form a stalk. Or grapes can be made of deal or any soft wood with a hole pierced through the centre large enough to admit of a leather or gutta percha stalk being drawn through and fastened at one end; they should now be stained and made into clusters; wooden grapes may be covered with damp skiver leather if preferred; it is necessary to observe, in making the clusters that the tying should be entirely concealed; all fruit and flowers must be stained, &c., precisely in the same manner as leaves.

TO ORNAMENT A FRAME.

Procure a deal frame of the size and form required, taking care to have it made of well-seasoned wood. Size it all over with patent size. Leave it about an hour to dry, then apply a coating of oak varnish stain, and when dry it will be ready for use. Commence the process of covering by attaching the stem with small tacks all round, in spaces of a few inches, in a zigzag direction. Supposing the vine pattern frame is selected, cover the wood with four or five gradations of foliage, well arranged, so as to preserve as nearly as possible, the natural appearance of the vine. Too great a profusion of grapes should be avoided ; but as the number and size of the clusters can hardly be determined, we must therefore leave it to the taste of the artist.

Common pins can be used with advantage in keeping in its proper place that portion of the work where glue only can be applied for the permanent fastening. When the work becomes firmly attached, the pins can either be withdrawn, or they can be cut off, close to the ornaments, with the nippers.

THE PROPER KIND OF FRAMES TO PROCURE.

The frames best adapted for the work, we have found to be those levelled off on the outer edge to about half an inch thinner than the inner, and formed as shewn in Fig. 1. Frames made in this shape greatly increase the

No. 2.

beauty of the entire design. A narrow gold beading we have generally added inside, as the gold gives a more finished appearance to the frame.

WATCH STANDS,

Can, like one below, be made by every carpenter; they must be strong to bear the nailing and gluing on of the leather ornaments.   The design here given (Fig. 2), we

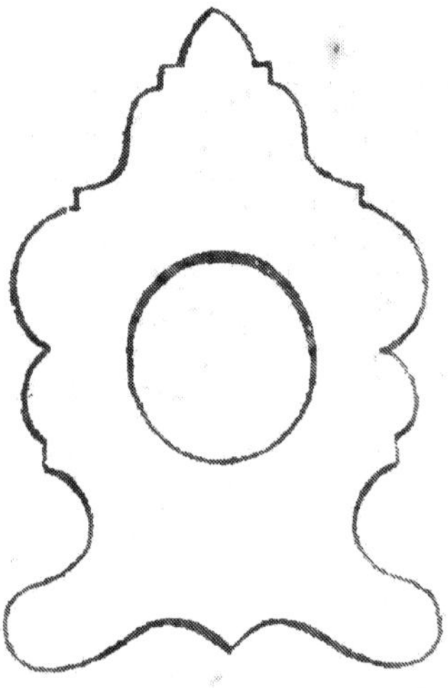

No. 3.

keep, as well as other descriptions in stock, but they can

be varied *ad infinitum;* and we shall be happy to make any design to order very promptly, or, as we have before observed, almost any carpenter can make them, if furnished with a drawing to work from.

THE WHITE LILY.

This beautiful flower, one of the oldest inhabitants of the flower garden, has six petals, which are formed of

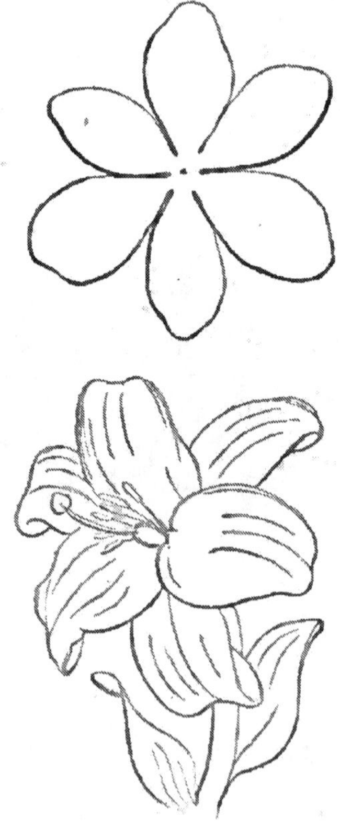

No. 4.

one piece of leather, as in Fig. 1; the three largest

petals, which, alternate with the others, are brought uppermost, while the three smaller ones are placed behind.   Our readers will at once perceive what is meant by referring to the finished flower ; they are to be veined and curled as in the natural flower, and the petals will require to be glued to keep them in their proper places ; it is necessary, if you have not our mould for that purpose, to adapt something to place the lily upon while modelling it, as near the shape of the interior of the flower as possible.   The lily has six stamina, with 'oblong anthers, which are made in the manner described for the convolvolus ; the pistil, with its swollen base or germen, lengthened style and heart-shaped stigma, should be carefully imitated from nature, being a very prominent feature in the flower ; the stamina should be placed round the germen of the pistil and fastened with liquid glue into the centre of the flower ; it must be recollected that the smooth side of the leather must be inside the lily as in the convolvolus ; some flowers require the smooth side of the leather inside, and some outside ; it must depend upon whether the interior or exterior of the flower is most in sight, and in some instances in the same flower some petals must be placed one way, and some another.

The bud of the lily is formed by merely folding the whole corolla together veined.

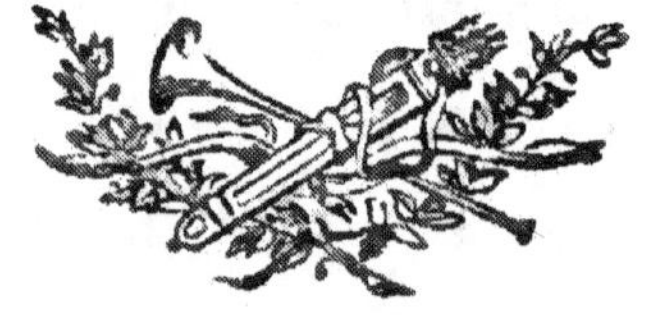

FUSCHIA.

—

The calyx forms the external part of this flower, and is made with one piece of leather cut as in the accompanying (Fig. 1.) The petals within this are four, and

No. 5.

are cut out, the four in one piece; in the form of the

dotted line, in Fig. 1, they must be moulded into shape and glued to the stamina inside the calyx so as to alternate with its petals. This flower belongs to the class Enneandria, having nine stamina ; they are to cut in one piece of leather. To put the fuschia together, proceed as follows :—Cut the nine stamina, and attach to them the wire, to form the stalk ; then roll the four petals firmly over the stamina ; they mnst be moulded and glued round the stamina and stalk, then take the calyx and roll round the whole ; the leaves must be expanded and moulded as in the engraving, taking care that the stamina are left out as in the natural flower, and that the inner petals alternate with the leaves of the calyx ; to make the buds, roll up the calyx, and turn the ends in, not inserting any stamina.

BRACKETS.

———

The beauty of a bracket depends entirely upon the artistic skill displayed in ornamenting it.   The engraving here given is to illustrate the form of bracket

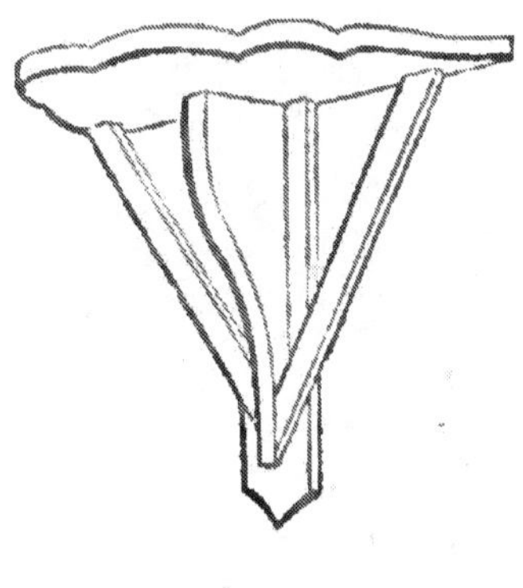

No. 6.

best suited to give it strength and solidity, and to aid the artist in bringing the work well out, the strips of wood on each side of the piece in the centre will be found exceedingly useful to nail and glue the work upon; they must be entirely covered with the foliage; the centre piece can be hidden or not to suit the design; the appearance of brackets are much improved by having the edge of the upper part gilded.

TO MAKE THE CONVOLVOLUS FLOWERS.

The Convolvolus, termed, by Botanists, Monopetalous, from its being composed of only one petal, is exceedingly well adapted for leather work; it is made by cutting a half circle of leather with a little piece cut out of the centre of the diameter, as seen in the annexed engraving (Fig. 1.)

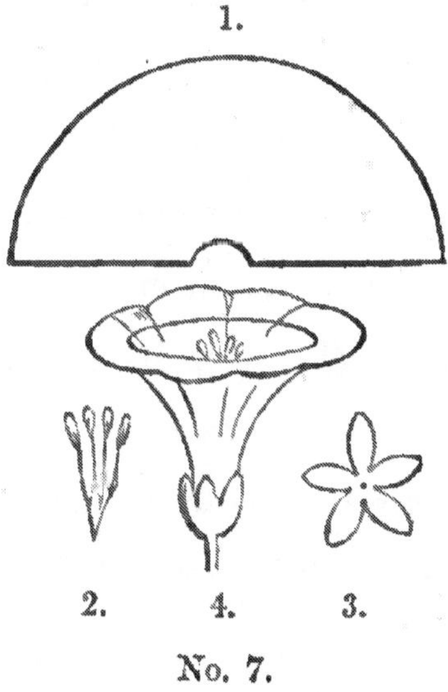

No. 7.

The leather so cut must be wetted and viened, then bent round (the smooth side inside, so that the smooth side of the leather form the inside of the flowers) until the two edges on each side of the notch come together, where they are to be joined by being either stitched or glued together ; it will then have a conical shape, and must be moulded with the fingers, or the mould, until it assumes a natural appearance ; the top can be cut to shape, and that part is finished ; cut the stamina, as in (Fig. 2.), leaving a stalk of leather attached to it in the following manner :—take a piece of basil about a quarter of an inch wide and a few inches long ; cut the top as in Fig. 2, taking care to preserve the form of the anther at the top of each stamen, and rolling the stalk part up, put it through the petal and glue it in its proper place. The calyx has five leaves (Fig. 3), and is cut in one piece of leather ; a hole is made in the centre, it is strung on the stalk and attached with glue to the bottom of the flower outside as in the finished flower (Fig. 4), so that the perfect convolvolus is composed of three pieces, the petal forming the body of the flower, the stamina inside, and the calyx at the bottom of the flower outside.

THE CONVOLVOLUS ANOTHER WAY.

Another way to make the Convolvolus is to cut a round piece of leather the size of the flower required, and while wet, moulding it over the mould for that purpose and bending it into shape ; the Canterbury bell can be formed of one piece of leather in the same manner, cutting the top into proper shape with a pair of scissors.

HOPS.

The Hop consists of numerous membraneous scales having the fruit within, and at their base; with the fruit however we have nothing to do, as it is out of sight. The membraneous scales are the petals of the flower, and in the engraving (Fig. 1,) are twenty in number;

Fig. 8.

they are all the same size, and are cut out of skiver leather, the shape of the single petal (Fig. 2).

D

To make the Hop, proceed as follows :—Take a piece
of wire and wind leather round the end of it, as in Fig. 3,
fastening it well with liquid glue; this inner body should
be somewhat shorter than the Hop is to be when completed, and pointed at both ends.   Cut out as many
petals as are requisite, and mould them into a convex
form at the end of each petal, then glue them alternately,
commencing at the bottom and finishing at the top of the
flowers.

PASSION FLOWER.

—

The Passion Flower is composed in leather of five pieces, and when well made presents a very beautiful specimen of what can be accomplished in that material.

In making the Passion Flower cut out the calyx of five

No. 9.

leaves—that is the part of the drawing in the annexed diagram with the pointed end ; then cut out the corolla of five petals with the rounded ends; cut also a circular piece for the nectary, which must be cut all round with the knife to form the radii,

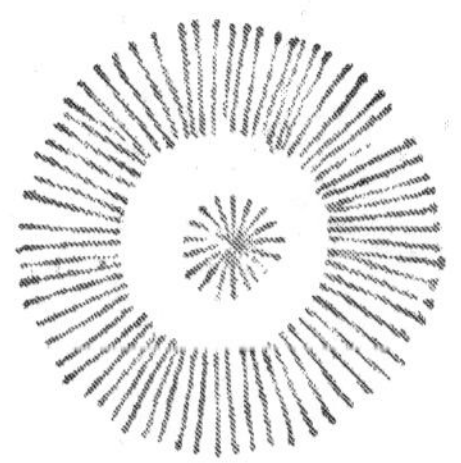

No. 10.

the centre having many small cuts radiating from the central point ; when turned upward, in putting it in its place, forms the fringe-like appearance around the pistil seen in the flowers.

The Passion Flower has five stamina with ladle-shaped ends, or anthers, and three stigmas a little elevated above and turning over the stamina; the anthers and stigma are made of one piece of leather. The involucrum is formed also of one piece, and the three leaves are laid one over the other as in the annexed flower.

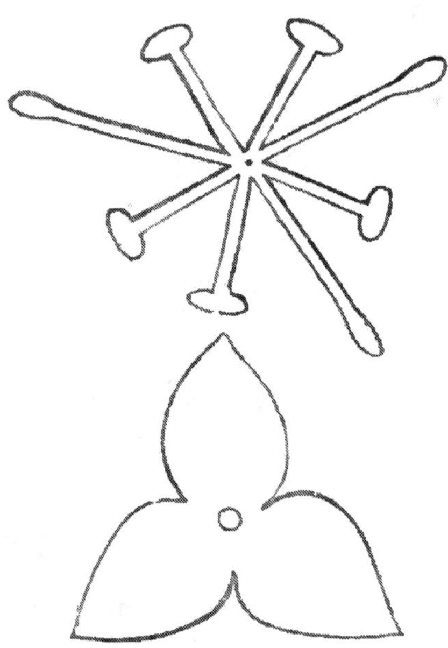

No. 11.

To put together the various parts above described and form the Passion Flower, begin by doubling a piece of wire over the angles of the stamina, twisting it underneath; roll a piece of skiver leather round the wire to form the style of the pistil and the stem of the whole flower; then turn up the three stigmas and roll a small piece of leather round them close to the stamina and turn them over; this being done, place the nectary on the stem, taking care that the cut portion in the centre be arranged upwards around the pistil. The petals are next placed on the stem, followed by the calyx; the leaves of the calyx must alternate with the petals; liquid glue must be inserted between each portion of the flower to give it firmness.

The involucrum, which is a sort of calyx, is put on the stem last a little way below the true calyx; we may just add, that all the leaves, petals, &c., with the exception of the involucrum, must have the smooth side of the leather uppermost; the petals and calyx must be hollowed out with the modelling tool for that purpose, or if that is not at hand, use the handle of the veining tool, and laying the petals and also the calyx on a smooth surface,

No. 12.

rub them with the ivory end of the veining tool till they become hollow and smooth as in the natural flower.

The above is the way, as plainly as we can possibly describe it, to make a Passion Flower. We have repeatedly made the flower exactly upon the above plan, and it has always been much admired.

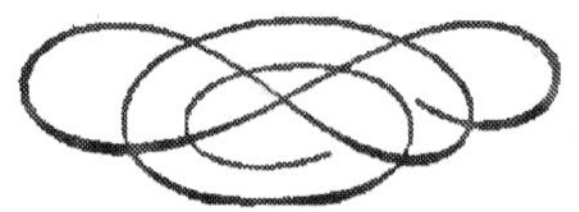

CAMILLA.

———

Camillas vary in the form of leaves, and the petals vary in number. To make a camillia, cut out two pieces, as in the annexed diagram, containing four petals in

No. 13.

each; then cut out one or two larger pieces, with six petals in each, and one or more still larger, with seven or eight petals; then, having a natural camilla at hand, mould them all into form, fasten all the pieces of leather together, the smallest at the top, and the largest at the bottom, so that the petals alternate, with liquid glue, and put a piece of wire through the whole for the stalk; cover it with skiver leather.

JESSAMINE.

To make the Jessamine, copy the corolla from the annexed design, by cutting a star-like piece of basil, into

No. 13.

which insert the wire for the stalk as closely as possible. As the stamina are not visible in this flower, it is needless to make them. The tube upon which the corolla rests, can be made by rolling a piece of leather round the wire thickest at the flower, and then add another piece of leather about an inch below the corolla, which must have five fine pointed leaves for the calyx.

DAISY.

—

The Daisy is formed by making two pieces of leather, like the pattern, one larger than the other, and putting

No. 14.

the wire, for stalk, through both of them. The little golden centre of the daisy, can be well imitated by placing a round piece of leather, rather thick, in the centre, shaved off at the edges, and marked wlth the veining tool full of dots.

ROSES.

—

A Wild Rose is made by cutting out two pieces of leather, exactly as in the engraving, putting the wire through two holes made in the centre of the pieces with a fine bradawl, and pass a piece of wire through the

No. 12.

holes, leaving both ends of the wire at the back to be twisted for the stalk. To form the stamina, cut fine strips of leather as long again as the stamina are required to be, and insert them under the eye of the wire which forms the stalk; then cut the stamina, and pinch them up into form; the top piece, containing five petals, must be moulded and curved upward, inclosing the stamina; the bottom piece also, containing five petals, must be moulded downwards, curving and bending them into form.

To make a larger Rose, cut out a smaller piece than is shewn in the engraving, of the same form, also the two in the engraving, and a larger piece of the same form making four pieces, containing twenty petals; then proceed as before-mentioned, and a fuller Rose is produced; thus the character of the flower and the number of petals can be regulated with comparative ease.

The rose leaves can be moulded at the back by pressing them into the grape mould with one of the pressing tools.

OAK AND IVY BRACKET.

The Bracket annexed is out of the usual run of brackets which have generally been ornamented with leather work. The vine and the convolvulus pattern are much used with very beautiful effect. We intended

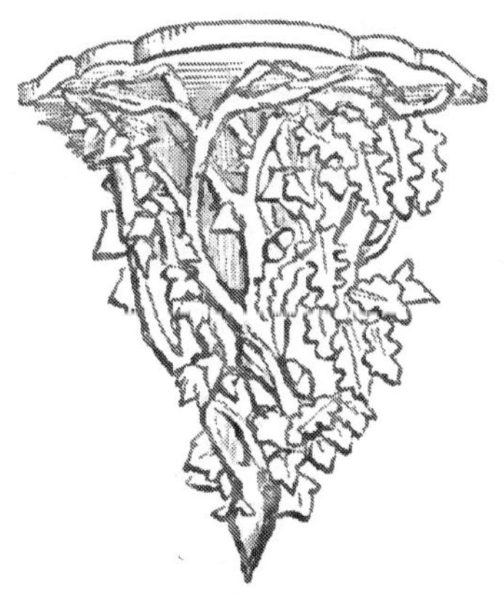

No. 15.

this design to exhibit old oak : it should be stained very dark, the oak stems being very thick, while the stems of ivy can be formed of tendrils. To make the oak stems get very thick wire, and have it cut to the desired lengths, then cover the wires with leather, and bend them to resemble knarled oak; attach, as naturally as possible, oak leaves and acorns at the back of the wires, and on the wood work as shewn in the skeleton bracket in a former part of this work; then attach the ivy tendrils, leaves, and berries around the oak stems, and the bracket is completed.

We have found it much improves the appearance of any piece of work we have been ornamenting, to give the whole when completed a slight coat of varnish.

WATCH STAND FINISHED.

The design for a Watch Stand will illustrate one of the various modes of ornamenting this kind of work; it is very light, and better than too much crowding the

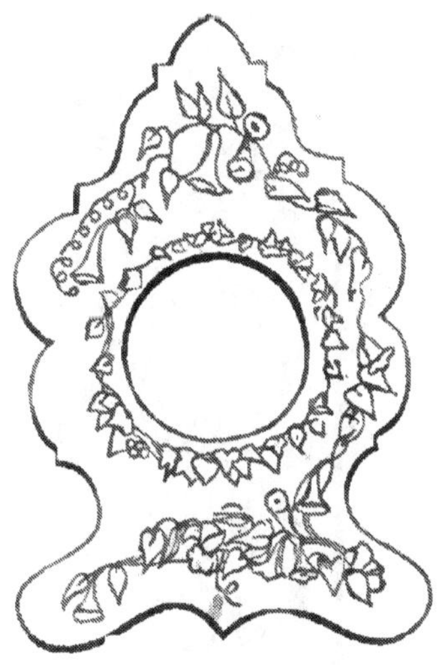

No. 16.

ornamented parts, which, besides being a waste of time, would not look so elegant as lighter work.

CARD RACKS

Can be made in a variety of ways—the design here

No. 17.

exhibited is novel, and at the same time very useful.

The back is made either with wood, or calf-skin leather; and the leaves forming the rack are also made of the same material. Calf-skin dries very hard, being treated exactly the same as the basil leather in the manner of working.

THE ROUND OPEN WORK FRAME.

The beautiful design in the accompanying page is made with a round frame of any width desired, having two rebates, one inside and one outside the frame—the inside rebate being to admit the picture, and the outside one to allow of the nailing firmly to the frame the open work, which is to be made in the following manner :— Take a flat board, an ironing board will do, lay the frame upon it, and with a black lead pencil or a piece of chalk, mark the size all round, making allowance for the rebate ; then having ready the stems, work them in and out, so as to form the open work as in the drawing ; when finished, nail it to the frame, and work stems and tendrils of the vine, hop, passion flower, or any other beautiful creeping plant, attaching the fruit or flowers in an artistic manner, and the result will be one of the most elegant frames ever beheld.

The open or trellis work of this frame should have stout wire enclosed in the basil leather, and in order that it may not appear formal, wind pieces of leather round the naked wire at irregular intervals to resemble knots, &c. then cover the whole with basil leather,—the stem and tendrils which are to wind in and out, and are a portion of the plant, are not to have wire in them.

Fire Screens are generally filled with Berlin wool, or some other fancy needlework. Those who would prefer to have an entire piece of leather work can paint landscapes or flowers upon white leather, using the same medium as is used in body color painting at the School of Design, mixed with finely powdered colors.

The basket ornamented with rose sprays outside, can be lined inside with velvet, and little pockets being

No. 19.

made in the velvet lining, they become a very useful article; the outside is stained old oak.

The running border here displayed can be adapted to

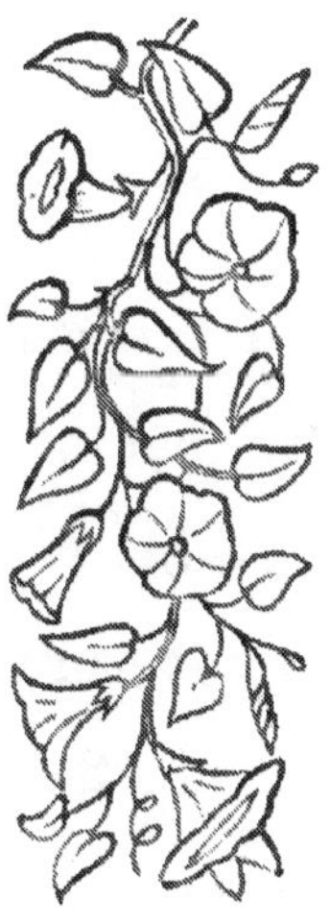

No. 20.

ornamenting cornices, poles, frames, &c. ; it is very easy of imitation, and will well repay the artist.

We shall conclude our designs with the table, which is made in four pieces, so that one part can be done at a time, and when completed, can be removed until the whole is completed, when it can be put firmly together, and forms a solid example of the use and beauty of the Ornamental Leather Work.

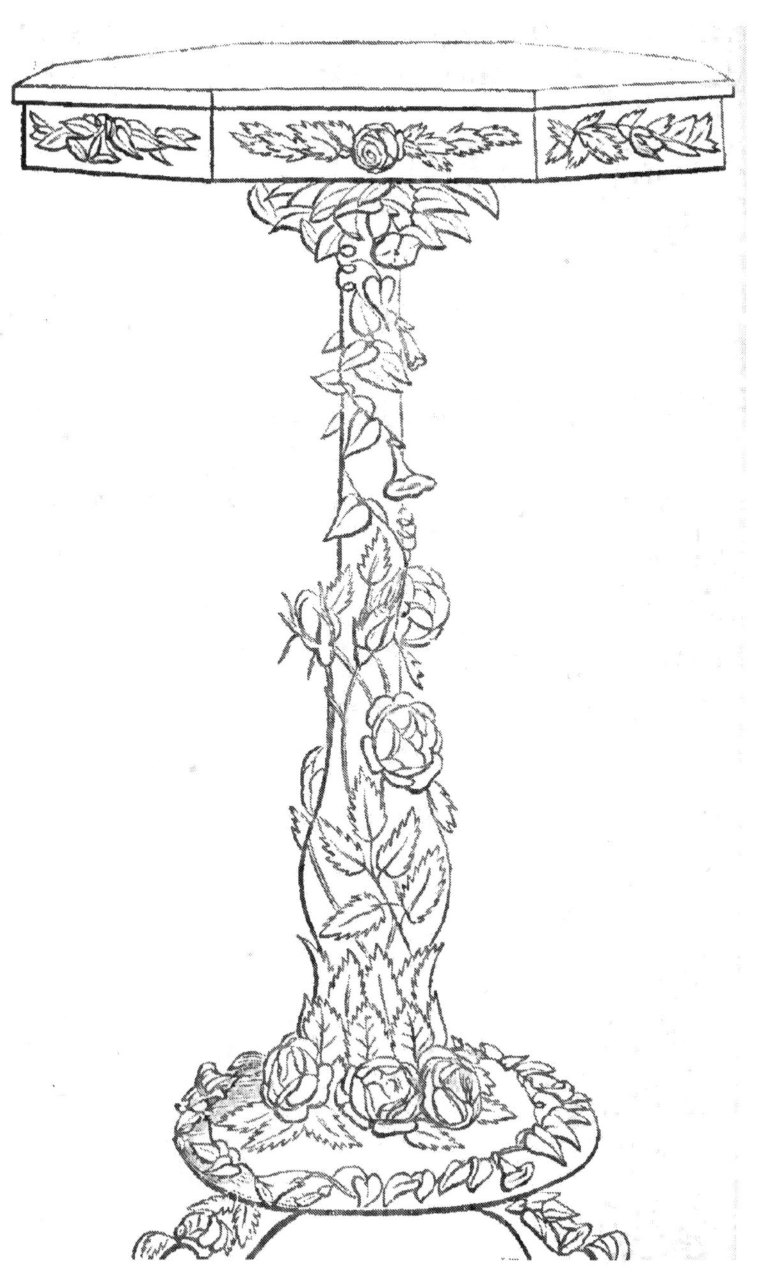

TO MAKE ACORNS.

Acorns can be made in the following manner. Procure some natural acorn-cups (which are to be found in great quantities in the autumn), choose such cups only as are perfectly sound; then pierce two holes through the bottom of the cup, pass a piece of fine wire through the holes, leaving the two ends long enough to be twisted into a stalk; if the stalk is to be exposed, it must be covered with skiver and made fast with Shaw's liquid glue. The most correctly-formed acorn tops are those turned in wood, which can be firmly placed in the cup by the aid of the liquid glue; this completes the fully-formed acorn.

CHERRIES.

———

Cherries are made in the same manner as grapes, and the stalk neatly covered with skiver leather.

APPLES, &c.

Apples and pears can be turned in wood; they may be left bare, or covered with skiver leather; they look much better covered with skiver, and are, then, leather work, properly speaking; or fruit may be moulded in plaster casts with gutta percha.

Carved wood figures may be draped with tolerable success with the skiver leather, but we have never seen any that looked well enough when finished to repay the time and trouble.

Recipes.

TO MAKE SIZE FOR STIFFENING THE LEATHER WORK.

Simmer 4 oz. of strips of parchment in 8 oz. of water till it is reduced one-half; skim off any impurities that may arise to the surface, then strain it through a fine sieve, or cloth, into a basin; leave it till cold, when it will be firm and clear; when required for use, cut off as much as you want, and warm it.   Use while warm.

TO MAKE STIFFENING WHICH IS NOT AFFECTED BY DAMP.

Mix, cold, 2 oz. of Australian red gum, 6 oz. of orange shellac, ½ pint spirits of wine; put all into a bottle, and shake it up occasionally till the gums are dissolved; strain, and it is fit for use. This is far preferable to the above size, as it is more hardening, dries quicker, is always ready for use, and is never affected by damp in change of weather.

TO MAKE MAHOGANY VARNISH STAIN, WHICH DRIES IN A FEW MINUTES.

Mix, cold, $\frac{3}{4}$ lb. Australian red gum, $\frac{1}{4}$ lb. garnet shellac, 1 pint spirits of wine; put them in a bottle, and shake occasionally, till the gum is dissolved; strain, and it is fit for use. The above makes a capital varnish for leather of all kinds, especially for the leather covers of old books; it preserves them, and gives an appearance almost equal to new.

SPIRIT OAK VARNISH STAIN

Can be made by adding to the above mahogany stain, a small portion of vegetable black, and shaking it up till well incorporated.   To use the spirit oak stain on larger surfaces we have found it preferable to apply it in the same manner as a French polish—namely, let all dirt and wax be perfectly rubbed off with fine glass paper, till quite smooth, then make a flannel rubber in the form of a printer's dabber, put a little stain on the dabber, and put a clean calico rag over it; apply a little linseed oil, with your finger, to the calico, and commence rubbing over a small space, in a circular direction (never suffering the rubber to remain on any part), till you feel it become tacky, then apply a little more oil, and so on, till the stain on the rubber is exhausted.   Should the stain become too thick to work freely, add a few drops of spirits of wine, and shake it well together. When you have raised a fine polish over the surface, let it remain a few hours to harden, then take a clean bit of calico, and just damp it with spirits of wine, rub it lightly over the surface in a circular direction, which, repeated two or three times, will clear off all smears, and leave the most beautiful gloss ever seen.

In this latter process of finishing off, you must be cautious not to damp the rag too much, for that would instantly destroy all the polish; also, to change the rag often, and not suffer it to remain on any part. For carved work it is only necessary to clean it as before directed, and apply the stain with a camel's-hair brush, by a gentle fire, letting it dry between each application.

The best oak varnish stain is that made with asphaltum; but, as the manufacturing is attended with great danger, we think it best not to give the particulars; and it can be procured cheaper than it could be made in small quantities.

TO PRESERVE LEAVES AND KEEP THEM IN FORM FOR IMITATION.

Procure 1 lb. or more of white starch powder, dry it well in an open dish before the fire, put it on one side to cool, when quite cool, put a layer of half an inch at the bottom of a small box, observing that the box also is dry; gather the leaves, if possible, on a fine summer day, and lay as many leaves gently on the starch powder at the bottom of the box as can be done without interfering with each other, then sprinkle starch powder over them, and shake it down so that the powder settles all round above and below the leaves until they are completely covered, and about half an inch of the starch powder above them, then put another layer of leaves, and proceed with the starch powder as before until the box is filled, then press the top part, quite full of starch powder, fastening the lid of the box firmly down until the leaves are required. Ferns and flat leaves can be preserved by placing them between sheets of blotting paper under a weight.

TO GILD LEATHER WORK.

The materials necessary for gilding of this kind are—

A Gilder's Knife.

A ditto Cushion.

Some Gold Leaf.

A little Cotton Wool.

A few Camel's Hair Pencils.

One or two Hog's Hair Tools.

A Tip.

Oil Gold Size.

Fat Oil.

Drying Oil, and a

Burnishing Stone.

They cost only a few shillings, and with care last a very long time.

Size the wood work twice over with parchment size, cut all the leaves, and make the flowers in the usual manner; size them all over twice with parchment size; nail them down to the frame, and glue them when tacks would look unsightly: needle points are very useful in this work to secure it firmly, and cut them short off when the glued parts are dry—all the flowers and leaves being attached, go over the entire work again with parchment size very thinly; the parchment size must be used warm; when the size is dry, mix well in a cup or any clean earthen vessel about an ounce of oil gold size, and with equal parts of fat oil and drying oil thin the gold size to the consistence of cream; take a hog's-hair tool, and with it brush equally and very thinly all over every part that can be seen with this prepared gold size, set it on one side for an hour or two or more, until it has become almost dry, and just sticks to your fingers when touched: it must now be gilded all over, and to do this, take a book of gold, handling it quietly, and mind there is no draft, as a current of air would blow all the gold away: turn out of the book two or three leaves of gold upon the cushion, and blow gently upon the centre of each leaf, to make them lay flat on the cushion; with the gilder's knife cut the gold leaves into the sizes required to cover the work, and with the tip or the gilder's knife take up the gold from the cushion and lay it all over the frame till it is covered, pressing the gold down with a large camel hair tool or a piece of cotton wool, taking care not to rub it backward or forward, but to put it very straight down on to the work; should there be any holes left, cut small pieces of gold leaf and lay over them, pressing the gold down, proceeding in the above manner till the frame is covered all over with gold; it must then be left to dry an hour or two, and when dry brush all the loose gold off with a large camel hair or badger's hair tool, and the gilding is completed. Leather work gilded by the above process will bear washing, and is the most durable kind of gilding known.

TO BURNISH GOLD.

Acorns and any wooden part attached to leather work
can be burnished, which adds much to the variety of the
work, and is done in the following manner :—that part
of the work intended to be burnished must be prepared
exactly as above, except that instead of using the prepared oil gold size take the white of an egg and give the
work a coat of it, let it dry, then give it another coat,
and when nearly dry see that it lays on evenly ; apply
the gold leaf all over ; leave it an hour or two to become
hard ; then burnish it by rubbing it all over with a bur-

nishing stone or any very hard and perfectly smooth substance. This burnish gilding is far more brilliant than the oil gold, but will not wash, and is not so durable.

BEE HIVES.

Bee Hives can be made with leather stems, as follows :
—Cut a piece of wood to the shape and size required ;
wind and glue upon it the stems, beginning at the top,
and finishing off at the bottom. To join the stems as
you proceed, cut each end to an angle, so that they fit ;
join them with liquid glue, and tie a piece of thread round
to hold them tightly together until the glue is dry.
When the hive is completed, that portion of thread left
visible can be cut off.

To imitate the tying seen in hives, mark with a pen,
or a camel's hair pencil, with the darkest stain, lines and
dots from top to bottom ; cut a small piece out of the
lower tier to make the entrance, and put a little handle
at the top with a piece of stem.

When made as above, on wood, and well glued, they can be sawn in halves, thus making two. Placed amongst foliage, frames, &c., they are quite in keeping, and have a pleasing effect.

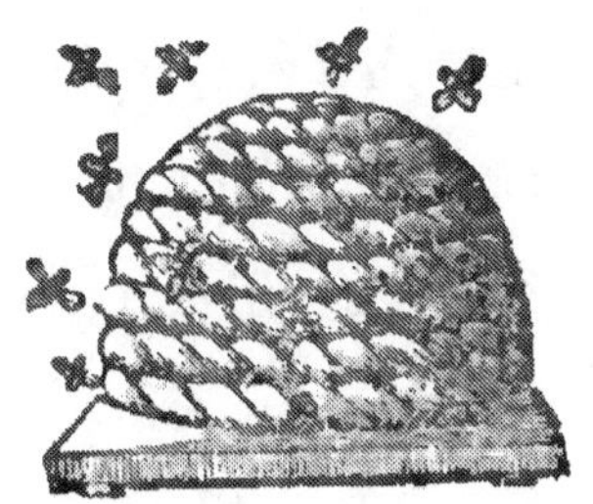

TO PAINT ORNAMENTAL LEATHER WORK.

Use finely powdered colours, and mix them to the consistence of cream, with the following medium :—Mix the white of an egg with 2 oz. of pure distilled vinegar; put them into a bottle and shake them well together whenever you are about to mix any colours with it: or mix the colours with parchment size warmed; use while warm: or mix them with a weak solution of gum arabic; and, in either case, varnish them with a quick drying pale varnish. Oil colours will not do for painting this kind of materials: any of the above mediums, properly prepared, will answer well. Gilding may be interspersed with brilliant effect.

A QUICK MODE OF STAINING.

The qucikest mode of staining the Ornamental Leather Work is as follows :—Procure a bottle of REVELL'S CHYMICAL OAK COLOUR STAIN. This preparation will not soil the hands, or the finest linen or woollen fabrics; will not stain wood or any other substance than the leather to which it is applied, to which it imparts the perfect appearance of old oak without any gloss, at the same time hardening the leather without injuring it.

DIRECTIONS FOR USE.

Having your leaves, &c., cut out and dried, pour some of the contents of this bottle into a saucer, and apply it copiously with a camel's hair brush, all over the leaves, back and front, particularly the edges ; bend them while damp as you wish them to appear upon the finished work, then dry them rather quickly at a moderate distance from the fire, or in a current of air ; when dry they are ready for use.

The leaves, &c., can be attached to any form of work, and it is completed. When the entire work is complete, it can be varnished at pleasure, as follows :—Procure a bottle of REVELL's OAK SPIRIT STAIN, and give the entire work an even coat of it; it dries in a few minutes, and has the appearance of polished oak.

TO STAIN WOODEN ARTICLES.

If all the work is to be left dull, give the frame or bracket, &c., a coat of OAK SPIRIT STAIN, which dries in dull if put upon new wood, not prepared in any manner. To prepare wooden frames, &c., so that the OAK SPIRIT STAIN shall assume a polished surface, it is necessary to size the frame well and leave it to dry; when dry, give it one or more coats of OAK SPIRIT STAIN.

Those who prefer making the Oak Spirit Stain, can do so by referring to the receipt in this book; it is made with little trouble, and is composed principally of Australian Red Gum; a new article to most of our readers; and, although many druggists, &c., have procured it when they have received orders for it, we are sorry to say, in several instances, they have said there was no article of that description; or else have substituted a different kind of gum, perfectly *worthless for this pur-pose;* consequently, disappointment has ensued; and in order to protect the public from being imposed upon, and ourselves the disgrace of publishing anything not practicable, we are obliged, in self-defence, to state how we came to use it.

In the month of January, 1852, the publisher was applied to for a varnish stain that would dry quickly, and at the same time be the colour required: he was making experiments for this purpose, when, taking up the TIMES newspaper of Friday, January 23rd, he found, under the heading of SOCIETY OF ARTS, an epitome of Professor EDWARD SOLLY's lecture, at the above Society on the previous Wednesday, on vegetable substances used in the Arts, &c. Allusions were made to a fine red gum from New South Wales: he procured the lecture, and then, after a little trouble, obtained samples; they were tested, and one was found to answer, and he has now in stock several tons of the proper kind for making the stain, and can supply it in any quantity.

We will now conclude by directing the student to an attentive observance of nature : we have avoided, as far as possible, technical terms ; where they are used the illustrations will, in most cases, explain them.   The study of this mode of decoration has often led those who had not before observed the varied beauties of the floral world to do so with the greatest pleasure and the happiest results.

SHAW'S LIQUID CLUE

Requires no preparation, sets almost immediately, will resist wet, violence, time, and climate; adheres to any surface or material; cements china, marble, wood, paper, leather, &c.; is useful to shipbuilders, carpenters, bookbinders, pianoforte, brush, and toy makers; and is so easy of application, that ladies and gentlemen may mend their own china, ornaments, toys, veneers, mouldings, parasols, book-covers, and a hundred other little articles, with the greatest ease and certainty.

Price 6d. and 1s. per Bottle.

SOLD WHOLESALE AND RETAIL BY

J. REVELL, 272, OXFORD STREET;

MESSRS. BARCLAY & Co., FARRINGDON STREET;

MESSRS. SUTTON & Co., BOW CHURCHYARD;

AND TO BE HAD OF ALL

OILMEN, CHEMISTS, FANCY STATIONERS,
&c., &c.

LIST OF MATERIALS, &c.,

FOR THE

ORNAMENTAL

LEATHER WORK.

SOLD BY

J. REVELL, 272, OXFORD STREET.

Basil Leather, of the first quality, at 1s. 6d. and 2s. per skin.

Skiver ditto, ditto, at   ditto.

Leather Leaves, 6d. per dozen, or 4s. per gross, assorted.

Leather Stems and Tendrils, 2d. each.

Passion Flowers, Roses, &c., from 6d. to 2s. 6d. each.

Convolvulus and other less elaborate Flowers, from 2d. each.

Holly and Ivy Berries, 6d. per bundle.

Acorns, 1s. per dozen.

Oak Varnish Stain, 1s. per bottle.

Spirit Oak   ditto, 1s.   ,,

Spirit Mahogany ditto, 1s. ,,

Revell's Chymical ditto, which possesses the property of staining the leather used for this work, and will not soil the finest linen, neither will it stain wood, or any other material than leather. It can be applied either cold or warm. Sold, with full directions for use accompanying each bottle, price 1s. This being the invention of the publisher, purchasers are requested to observe his name and address on each seal.

Stephens' Wood Stains.

Stains and Varnishes of every description.

Saucers for the Oak Stain, &c., 1s. per doz.

Shaw's Liquid Glue, without smell, 1s. per bottle.

Ditto, Old kind, 6d.   ,,

Prepared Stiffening, 1s.   ,,

Veining Tools, 1s. 6d. each.

Cutting ditto, 1s.   ,,

Grape Moulds, 2s. 6d. per set.

Bradawls, 6d. each.

Hammers, 1s. 3d. ,,

Wire of different sizes.

Hog's Hair Brushes, 3d. to 6d. each.

Camel's Hair Pencils, from 1d.   ,,

And a variety of Brackets, Frames, &c., for Ornamenting.

Printed by S. Odell, 18, Princes Street, Cavendish Square.

Oil Colours in Patent Collapsible Tubes,

Of various sizes, and in Extra Fine Powder.

Cremnitz White	Purple Madder
Flake White	Light Red
Nottingham White	Venetian Red
Ultramarine	Indian Red, 1, 2
Ultramarine Ashes	Brown Red
Cobalt	Raw Sienna
Royal Smalt	Burnt Sienna
French Ultramarine	Brown Ochre
Permanent Blue	Burnt Brown Ochre
Antwerp Blue	Roman Ochre
Prussian Blue	Burnt Roman Ochre
Indigo	Vandyke Brown
Yellow Ochre	Raw Umber
Indian Yellow	Burnt Umber
Chrome, 1, 2, 3	Brown Pink
Italian Pink	Madder Brown
Yellow Lake	Cologne Earth
King's Yellow	Bone Brown
Lemon Yellow, 1, 2	Cappa Brown
Dutch Pink	Asphaltum
Naples Yellow	Bitumen
Lake	Mummy
Purple Lake	Emerald Green
Indian Lake	Verdigris
Crimson Lake	Terra Vert
Scarlet Lake	Chrome Green, 1, 2, 3
Chinese Vermillion	Oxyde of Chromium
Orange Vermillion	Ivory Black
Red Chrome	Blue Black
Carmine	Lamp Black
Madder Lake	Sugar of Lead
Rose Madder	Gumption
Pink Madder	Magylph

Sable Hair Pencils.

For Oil or Water.

Large Goose, Brown or Red
Small   ditto   ditto
Duck   ditto
Crow   ditto
Small Swan
Large ditto
Miniature
Lining or Rigging
Writing and Striping

French Sables.

IN TIN FOR WATER.
Red or Brown.
Nos. 1, 2, 3, 4, 5, 6.

Sables for Oil.

Round & Flat.
Nos. 1,2,3,4,5,6,7,8,9,10,11,12.

French Brushes.

Flat & Round.
Nos. 1,2,3,4,5,6,7,8,9, 10,11,12.

Camel Hair Pencils,

All Sizes, Long and Short.

Camel Hair Brushes,

In Flat Tins.

$\frac{1}{2}$ inch	$1\frac{1}{4}$ inch
$\frac{3}{4}$,,	2 ,,
1 ,,	$2\frac{1}{2}$,,
$1\frac{1}{4}$,,	3 ,,
$1\frac{1}{2}$,,	4 ,,

Camel Hair Brushes.

In Round Tins.
Nos. 1, 2, 3, 4, 5, 6, 7, 8.

Pencil Sticks.

Cedar, Ebony, Ivory,
6, 12 & 15 in.

Badger Softeners.

Round & Flat.
Nos. 1,2,3,4,5,6,7,8,9,10,11,12.

Palette Knives.

Horn and Ivory
Steel, with Horn or Bone Handles
  Do.   Ivory Handles
  Do. Spatula Shape, Horn
    Handles
  Do.   ditto   Ivory   do.

Port Crayons.

Steel, Albata, and Brass.

Brush Washers for Turpentine.

Nos, 1, 2, 3, 4.

Oils and Varnish.

Spirits Turpentine
Cold Drawn Linseed Oil
Nut and Poppy Oil
Drying Oil, pale or strong
Fat Oil
Japan Gold Size
Mastic Varnish
Copal Varnish
White Hard Spirit Varnish
Asphaltum
Magylph
Gumption

Extra Fine Cake and Moist Water Colors,

IN CAKES AND HALF CAKES.

Permanent White	Lake
Constant White	Crimson Lake
Flake White	Scarlet Lake
Chinese White	Dark Lake
	Indian Lake
Ultramarine	Vermillion
Ultramarine Ashes	Extract Vermillion
Cobalt	Scarlet Vermillion
Azure Blue	Carmine
Royal Smalt	Burnt Carmine
French Ultramarine	Dragon's Blood
Permanent Blue	Madder Lake
Antwerp Blue	Rose Madder
Prussian Blue	Pink Madder
Indigo	Pure Scarlet
Intense Blue	Dahlia Carmine
French Blue	Indian Red
	Light Red
Gamboge	Venetian Red
Yellow Ochre	Brown Red
Indian Yellow	Red Orpiment
Platina Yellow	Red Chalk
Gall Stone	Red Chrome
Lemon Yellow	Deep Rose
Chrome, 1, 2, 3	
Italian Pink	Raw Sienna
Dutch Pink	Burnt Sienna
Yellow Lake	Brown Ochre
Mars Yellow	Roman Ochre
King's Yellow	Burnt Roman Ochre
Naples Yellow	Vandyke Brown
Patent Yellow	Verona Brown, 1, 2, 3
	Sepia
Orange Orpiment	Warm Sepia
Orange Red	Roman Sepia
Mars Orange	Raw Umber
Orange Vermillion	Burnt Umber

Water Colors, *(continued.)*

<table>
<tr><td>

Brown Pink
Madder Brown
Cologne Earth
Bone Brown
Bronze
Reuben's Brown
Mars Brown
Intense Brown
Cappa Brown
Bistre
Chalons Brown

Payne's Grey
Neutral Tint

Purple
Indian Purple
Purple Madder
Purple Lake

</td><td>

Sap Green
Emerald Green
Prussian Green
Chrome Green, 1, 2, 3
Oxyde of Chrome
Verdigris
Barber's Green
Sea Green
Dark Green
Hooker's Green, 1, 2
Olive Green
Terra Vert
Green Bice
Lamp Black
Ivory Black
Blue Black
British Ink
Inlaying Black

</td></tr>
</table>

Gold and Silver Shells.

Indelible, and Bright's Landscape Crayons.

Singly or in Sets.

Chalks, Crayons.

Italian Black Chalk
Ditto Red and White
Soft French Black
Charcoal
Pastiles
Black Square Conté Crayons
Ditto, Round, plain ditto
Ditto, Glazed   ditto
Velours, (very Soft and Black)
Round and Square Red Conté
Bistre

Lead Pencils,

Extra Prepared.

H. Hard, for Sketching
H.H. Harder, for Outlines, &c.
H.H.H. Very Hard, for Archi-
    tectural Drawing, &c.
H.B. Hard and Black
E.H.B. Extra Hard and Black
B. Black for Shading
B.B. Soft and Black
E.B.B. Extra Soft and Black
F. Fine for General Drawing

Earthenware.

Palettes and Saucers
Cabinet Saucers in Morocco
    Case

<h2 style="text-align:center">Miscellaneous.</h2>

Drawing Pins	Gold Leaf
Indian Ink	Mezzotint Brushes
Indian Rubber	Permanent Ink
Indian Glue	Velvet Scrubs
Sponge	Picture Frames
Ox Gall	Sealing Wax and Wafers
Lithograph Chalk	Pink Saucers
Gilder's Knives, Tips and Cushions	Slate Pencils
Poonah Brushes	Tracing Points
Burnish Gold Size	Burnishing Stones
Oil ditto	Bronze
	Graining Combs and Tools

<h3 style="text-align:center">Revell's Permanent Brown Ink,</h3>

FOR DRAWING UPON BASIL LEATHER.

Price 1s. per Bottle.

Pen and Ink Drawings can be made with this Ink, they have all the appearance of the so-called Poker Paintings, (viz. Drawings upon Wood, executed with one or more red hot wires.) The Ink is permanent, and will be found advantageous as an adjunct to the Ornamental Leather Work.

<h3 style="text-align:center">Unprepared Colours of the First Quality.</h3>

Colours of every description for House Painting, Park Fencing, &c.

www.ingramcontent.com/pod-product-compliance
Lightning Source LLC
Chambersburg PA
CBHW061034050726
47592CB00004B/1438